RZIM Critical Questions Discussion Guides

Who Was
Jesus?

Scot McKnight

SERIES EDITOR Ravi Zacharias
GENERAL EDITOR Danielle DuRant

Inter-Varsity Press
Nottingham, England

IVP Connect
An imprint of InterVarsity Press
Downers Grove, Illinois

InterVarsity Press
P.O. Box 1400, Downers Grove, IL 60515-1426
World Wide Web: www.ivpress.com
Email: email@ivpress.com

Inter-Varsity Press, England
Norton Street, Nottingham NG7 3HR, England
Website: www.ivpbooks.com
Email: ivp@ivpbooks.com

Published in association with the literary agency of Wolgemuth & Associates, Inc., Orlando, Florida.

InterVarsity Press® *is the book-publishing division of InterVarsity Christian Fellowship/USA*®, *a student movement active on campus at hundreds of universities, colleges and schools of nursing in the United States of America, and a member movement of the International Fellowship of Evangelical Students. For information about local and regional activities, write Public Relations Dept., InterVarsity Christian Fellowship/USA, 6400 Schroeder Rd., P.O. Box 7895, Madison, WI 53707-7895, or visit the IVCF website at <www.intervarsity.org>.*

Inter-Varsity Press, England, is closely linked with the Universities and Colleges Christian Fellowship, a student movement connecting Christian Unions in universities and colleges throughout Great Britain, and a member movement of the International Fellowship of Evangelical Students. Website: www.uccf.org.uk.

All Scripture quotations, unless otherwise indicated, are taken from the Holy Bible, New International Version®. NIV®. *Copyright* ©1973, 1978, 1984 by International Bible Society. Used by permission of Zondervan Publishing House. All rights reserved.

Adapted from Who Was Jesus? *by Scot McKnight (Norcross, Ga.: RZIM, 2002).*

Design: Cindy Kiple
Images: David Buffington/Getty Images

USA ISBN 978-0-8308-3153-1
UK ISBN 978-1-84474-224-0

Printed in the United States of America ∞

P	19	18	17	16	15	14	13	12	11	10	9	8	7	6	5	4	3	2	1
Y	23	22	21	20	19	18	17	16	15	14	13	12	11	10	09	08	07			

Contents

Introduction

I was at an airport looking for my departure gate, and I noticed that the flight listed was to another city. So I asked a passenger if that flight was headed to Atlanta or elsewhere. She promptly answered my question and told me the notation was wrong. As I thanked her and turned to find a seat, she said, "Are you Ravi Zacharias?" I answered yes. Then came this utterly surprising response: "I listen to you on the radio regularly. I didn't know you had questions as well." I laughed at her compliment and assured her that I had several questions, especially if I want to get to the right destination.

There are so many answers out there and a question to every answer. To ask them is to engage with information. To ask questions about life's ultimate questions is to be in the pursuit of God. That's what this series is about: to take you to the heart and mind of God, which is the right destination.

In this series, critical questions raised by thinking minds are answered by those who have asked them themselves, and found the answer in the person and teaching of Jesus Christ. There are writers in this series that I have heavily leaned on myself. They are trained in the art of critical thinking not merely for the intellectual stimulation it brings but for the ultimate pursuit: the bridge between the heart and the mind so that thinking shapes being, which in turn impels doing.

In our time such helps as this series are invaluable. On every side, be it the academy or the movies, just enough doubt is cast on the person of Jesus that minds are left unsteadied in their trust in the Scriptures and the truth claims of the gospel. Such doubts and questionings are rarely answered by a one-blow argument. Life is not as simple as that. In fact, any worldview that depends on one such knockout argument flirts with logical and experiential extinction.

Life closes in on us from multiple sides. That is why a good apologetic starts with the fundamentals before it deals with the specifics. From the nature of truth to the incarnation of it in Jesus, from the trustworthiness of the Scriptures to the questions of moral reasoning, they are addressed here. These succinct and interactive discussion guides will stir your mind and occupy a much-used section in your library.

I sincerely hope this series will be both a tool of equipment and a source of inspiration. Darrell Bock in his study *Can I Trust the Bible?* sums up the content of these slender volumes well:

> If there is the possibility that God has spoken through this text and has participated in the history it records, then the answers to our questions are not a mere academic exercise. Our journey back into these seemingly foreign, ancient times may be a real opportunity to see more clearly who we are and were created to be.

A couple words of appreciation are well in order. First, the original effort in putting this all together was done by Paul Copan. In this instance, the hard work as general editor is by Danielle DuRant, who labored long to make this accessible. I am also grateful to InterVarsity Press for seeing the value in this short series and taking the step to publish it. Those of us who study this material will be the beneficiaries.

Questions will haunt as long as the mind is alive. The answers of Christ will inspire and instruct because he is the author of life.

Ravi Zacharias

Getting the Most Out of This Guide

The best way to learn something about a significant historical figure," suggests Scot McKnight in the opening paragraph of his booklet *Who Was Jesus?* (Norcross, Ga.: RZIM, 2002), "is to ask the person himself *and* those who know that person best." Thus he takes notice of the crowds who followed Jesus, his opponents, and his closest followers, the disciples.

In this study guide we will do the same. We will especially consider the expectations of those who encountered Jesus and the ways Jesus met—and often challenged—these expectations. Finally, we ourselves will step into his story, as it were, to hear his words to us, words that compel us to ask who this Jesus really is.

■ SUGGESTIONS FOR INDIVIDUAL STUDY

1. As you begin each session, pray that God will speak to you through his Word.

2. Read the introduction to the session and respond to the opening reflection question or exercise. This is designed to help you focus on God and on the theme of the session.

3. Each session considers a particular passage or passages of Scripture, and is supplemented by the author's commentary. Read and reread the text before engaging the questions.

4. Write your answers to the questions in the spaces provided or in a personal journal. Writing can bring clarity and deeper understanding of yourself and of God's Word.

5. It might be good to have a Bible dictionary handy. Use it to look up any unfamiliar words, names or places.

■ SUGGESTIONS FOR MEMBERS OF A GROUP STUDY

1. Come to the study prepared. Follow the suggestions for individual study mentioned above. You will find that careful preparation will greatly enrich your time spent in group discussion.

2. Be willing to participate in the discussion. The leader of your group will not be lecturing. Instead, he or she will be encouraging the members of the group to discuss what they have learned. The leader will be asking the questions that are found in this guide.

3. Stick to the topic being discussed. Your answers should be based on the texts provided and not on outside authorities such as commentaries or speakers. Only rarely should you refer to other portions of the Bible. This allows for everyone to participate in in-depth study on equal ground.

4. Be sensitive to the other members of the group. Listen attentively when they describe what they have learned. You may be surprised by their insights! Each question assumes a variety of answers. Many questions do not have "right" answers, particularly questions that aim at meaning or application. Instead the questions push us to explore the topic more thoroughly. When possible, link what you say to the comments of others. Also, be affirming whenever you can. This will encourage some of the more hesitant members of the group to participate.

5. Be careful not to dominate the discussion. We are sometimes so eager to express our thoughts that we leave too little opportunity for others to respond. By all means participate! But allow others to also.

6. Expect God to teach you through the material being discussed and through the other members of the group. Pray that you will have an enjoyable and profitable time together, but also that as a result of the study you will find ways that you can take action individually and/or as a group.

7. Remember that anything said in the group is considered confidential and should not be discussed outside the group unless specific permission is given to do so.

8. If you are the group leader, you will find additional suggestions at the back of the guide.

1 Meeting Jesus

Hands down, the best way to learn something about a significant historical figure is to ask the person himself *and* those who know that person best. In the case of Jesus, since we have no access to him directly (all information comes to us secondhand), we will have to ask a set of relevant persons. These would include (but not be limited to) the *crowds* who witnessed him, the *opponents* who thought less of him than did his followers, and then finally from his closest followers, the *disciples*.

■ OPEN

Talk about a person you have been wanting to meet—an accomplished athlete, leader or person a friend knows. What draws you to this person?

■ STUDY

Jesus' healing of a paralytic man is perhaps familiar, namely because the man's friends lower him through the roof of a house. Both Mark and Luke tell us the reason for their desperation: "they could not get him to Jesus because of the crowd" (Mark 2:4; cf. Luke 5:19). Throughout the Gospels we read of various crowds who encounter Jesus. One theme emerges: he elicits their attention and a marked response, whether awe or anger. Though he did not seek notice, Jesus' words and miracles drew crowds wherever he went. **Read Mark 2:1-12.**

¹*A few days later, when Jesus again entered Capernaum, the people heard that he had come home. ²So many gathered that there was no room left, not even outside the door, and he preached the word to them. ³Some men came, bringing to him a paralytic, carried by four of them. ⁴Since they could not get him to Jesus because of the crowd, they made an opening in the roof above Jesus and, after digging through it, lowered the mat the paralyzed man was lying on. ⁵When Jesus saw their faith, he said to the paralytic, "Son, your sins are forgiven."*

⁶*Now some teachers of the law were sitting there, thinking to themselves, ⁷"Why does this fellow talk like that? He's blaspheming! Who can forgive sins but God alone?"*

⁸*Immediately Jesus knew in his spirit that this was what they were thinking in their hearts, and he said to them, "Why are you thinking these things? ⁹Which is easier: to say to the paralytic, 'Your sins are forgiven,' or to say, 'Get up, take your mat and walk'? ¹⁰But that you may know that the Son of Man has authority on earth to forgive sins. . . ."* He said to the paralytic, ¹¹*"I tell you, get up, take your mat and go home." ¹²He got up, took his mat and walked out in full view of them all. This amazed everyone and they praised God, saying, "We have never seen anything like this!"*

1. How do the people respond when they hear of Jesus' arrival in Capernaum?

What does Jesus do (see verses 1, 2)?

2. The crowds see the paralytic man lowered from the roof, yet Mark tells us that Jesus sees something more. What does Jesus see?

3. Imagine you were among the crowd in this room. What do you think would be your first impression of Jesus' reply to the man (verse 5)?

If there were crowds and if Jesus made a stir with his actions and his sayings, then it is likely that people in the crowds offered evaluations. More importantly, it is notable that the "Christology" of the crowds (their theological understanding of the person and work of Christ) is "low" (less than a full confession of Jesus as Son of God) and in some senses not what the Evangelists themselves put forward as their own Christology. Since the "Christology" of the crowds is appreciably lower than early Christian theology of the Evangelist (where Jesus was confessed to be Son of God and even divine), it is *more likely* that the Evangelist did *not* make up this "crowd Christology." Had he made it up, it would have looked more like his own theology.

We have then in the reports of the crowds seeing Jesus' healings and hearing his teachings what amounts to an eyewitness testimony.

There is a consistent testimony in the Gospel stories that those who saw Jesus' healings, and sometimes those who heard him teach, were *impressed at a profound level* at what they saw and what they heard. Those who saw Jesus' healings would have felt the presence of the numinous or a sacred mystery. We are not asking for too much here; this is how humans respond whenever they encounter what appears to be the supernatural. They experience wonder (Matthew 8:27), astonishment (Mark 1:27), amazement (2:12), fear (4:41), or dumbfoundedness (7:37). The experience of wonder in the presence of an unusual occurrence is common to ancients and moderns. *If* Jesus did miracles, and *if* the crowds saw them, then it is certain that the crowds would have been amazed.

4. Why is it reasonable to believe that the crowds' observations and comments about Jesus are in keeping with what occurred?

5. Why would amazement be an appropriate reaction to Jesus' miracles?

6. Look again at the passage from Mark. Why do the teachers of the law become upset? Explain why they would reach this conclusion.

7. According to Jesus, what is the purpose of his healing ministry (verse 10)?

What does his statement tell us about who he claims to be and what we might expect as we continue to study his life and ministry?

The friends of this paralyzed man did everything they could to bring him within the sight and touch of Jesus. They even disfigured the property of the person in whose house Jesus was visiting in the hope that he would perform a miracle for their friend. I suspect they must have reasoned that if Jesus could make a paralyzed man walk again, then replacing a roof would be a minor problem. But as they lowered this man within reach of the Savior, they were not expecting an apologetic discussion.

"Which of the two is harder," asked the Lord, "to bring physical healing or to forgive a person's sins?" The irresistible answer was self-evident, was it not? *To bring physical healing* because that would be such a miraculous thing, visible to the naked eye. The invisible act of forgiveness had far less evidentiary value. Yet, as they pondered and as we ponder, we discover repeatedly in life that the logic of God is so different to the logic of humanity. We move from the material to the spiritual in terms of the spectacular, but God moves from the spiritual to the material in terms of the *essential*. . . .

In this instance, Jesus followed the act of forgiveness with the easier act of physical healing so that the paralyzed man

> would feel the touch of the Savior from what was more mean-
> ingful to what was more felt. If he was a wise man he would
> walk with the awareness that the apparently less visible mira-
> cle was actually more miraculous than the more visible one—
> but his feeling of gratitude for his restored body would remain
> a constant reminder to him of the restoration of his soul.[1]

8. Can you think of an instance in your own life when you
sought a miracle or instant relief from the sometimes hard
road of daily living?

9. The Scriptures tell us that though God can and does perform
miracles, he is also committed to our perseverance and character, which are forged in life's trials. Do you find it difficult
to balance these two perspectives?

10. What does the passage above suggest is the ultimate miracle?
Why?

11. Mark tells us everyone present responded in two ways after
Jesus heals the paralytic man (verse 12). How might you main-
tain a sense of amazement and praise throughout the week?

---

[1]Ravi Zacharias, "Apologetics: Shadow or Reality?" *Just Thinking*, fall 2004 (available online at
www.rzim.org/publications/jttran.php?seqid=98).

■ GOING FURTHER

This biblical passage suggests that nothing could obstruct the paralytic man and his friends from seeking an audience with Jesus. Have you ever known such passion for God? What motivates you in your efforts? What hinders you? You may want to take time to write about these reflections.

Additional Reading

For a good introduction to the life and ministry of Jesus see F. F. Bruce's classic work *Jesus: Lord & Savior* (Downers Grove, Ill.: InterVarsity Press, 1986).

LUKE 7:11-23, 36-50

That Jesus' teachings evoked amazement is witnessed to, and that Jesus taught things that were unusual, and that he made out-of-the ordinary claims on other matters (e.g., Luke 9:57-62) cannot be questioned. These are the warp and woof of Jesus' entire mission. That Jesus' teachings stood out from the ordinary scribes and took direct issue with the Sadducees is quite reasonable. Additionally, as a result of seeing Jesus' actions and hearing his teachings, the crowds on a few occasions came to the conclusion that Jesus was a "prophet."

■ OPEN

Recall a time when you anticipated a new job, long-planned vacation or unfamiliar experience, such as a marathon or wedding. What were some of your expectations and feelings before and after the event? Were you surprised by some things you encountered? How did this experience surpass your expectations?

■ STUDY

The Gospel writers each record instances of perhaps the most amazing miracle that the crowds witness Jesus perform: the raising of a person from the dead. In Matthew, Mark and Luke we see Jesus raise the daughter of a synagogue ruler, and in John, Lazarus is brought back to life after being dead for four days. Luke 7 concerns a widow's only son. When John the Baptist learns of this miracle, he sends messengers to ask Jesus if he indeed is the one—the Messiah—whom he was to expect. John's expectations of him are challenged because John is suffering in prison, just as a Pharisee's perspective is later tested when he sees a woman anoint Jesus. **Read Luke 7:11-23.**

^{11}*Soon afterward, Jesus went to a town called Nain, and his disciples and a large crowd went along with him.* ^{12}*As he approached the town gate, a dead person was being carried out—the only son of his mother, and she was a widow. And a large crowd from the town was with her.* ^{13}*When the Lord saw her, his heart went out to her and he said, "Don't cry."*

^{14}*Then he went up and touched the coffin, and those carrying it stood still. He said, "Young man, I say to you, get up!"* ^{15}*The dead man sat up and began to talk, and Jesus gave him back to his mother.*

^{16}*They were all filled with awe and praised God. "A great prophet has appeared among us," they said. "God has come to help his people."* ^{17}*This news about Jesus spread throughout Judea and the surrounding country.*

^{18}*John's disciples told him about all these things. Calling two of them,* ^{19}*he sent them to the Lord to ask, "Are you the one who was to come, or should we expect someone else?"*

^{20}*When the men came to Jesus, they said, "John the Baptist sent us to you to ask, 'Are you the one who was to come, or should we expect someone else?'"*

^{21}*At that very time Jesus cured many who had diseases, sicknesses and evil spirits, and gave sight to many who were blind.* ^{22}*So he replied to the messengers, "Go back and report to John what you have seen and heard: The blind receive sight, the lame walk, those who have leprosy*

are cured, the deaf hear, the dead are raised, and the good news is
preached to the poor. ²³*Blessed is the man who does not fall away on*
account of me."

1. Describe Jesus' immediate response to the situation he encounters at the town gate.

2. Unless an individual was family or close to the deceased, one
   would never touch a coffin, as Jewish tradition pronounced
   such a person unclean. What does this insight, as well as the
   subsequent miracle, tell us about Jesus?

3. Notice the crowd's statements after Jesus raises the young
   man to life. What were their expectations of a prophet of
   God?

4. Recall a time when, because of your circumstances, you
   doubted God. How did you begin to deal with your questions?

5. How would you characterize Jesus' reply to John's messengers?

How does what they "have seen and heard" attest to them—
and to us—of Jesus' uniqueness and authority?

Scholars have recently undertaken to define the variety of
prophets in the ancient Jewish world. To summarize what is
otherwise a very complex discussion, it is highly likely that
the crowds would have recognized Jesus at least as a *popular
leadership prophet.* This means they would have seen Jesus as
*standing between God and the people, revealing God's message
to the people* and *calling the people to repent to avoid disaster
and doom.* Furthermore, they would have seen him as more
than a "voice": Jesus not only *spoke* but *led his followers into
a movement.* That is, Jesus' kind of prophetic ministry was intent on shaping a new society around himself.

Jesus described the response to his own ministry as the
same kind of response to Israel's prophets—that is, he would
die at the hands of those who opposed his message (Luke
13:33). Further, he said that his own disciples would be
treated as were the ancient prophets. It is no surprise then
when the crowds arrive at the conclusion that Jesus must be
a prophet.

6. How is Jesus' prophetic ministry similar to and yet also different from that of some Old Testament prophets?

7. According to the passage above, what were the crowds' expectations of Jesus as a prophet?

Read Luke 7:36-50.

[36]Now one of the Pharisees invited Jesus to have dinner with him, so he went to the Pharisee's house and reclined at the table. [37]When a woman who had lived a sinful life in that town learned that Jesus was eating at the Pharisee's house, she brought an alabaster jar of perfume, [38]and as she stood behind him at his feet weeping, she began to wet his feet with her tears. Then she wiped them with her hair, kissed them and poured perfume on them.

[39]When the Pharisee who had invited him saw this, he said to himself, "If this man were a prophet, he would know who is touching him and what kind of woman she is—that she is a sinner."

[40]Jesus answered him, "Simon, I have something to tell you."

"Tell me, teacher," he said.

[41]"Two men owed money to a certain moneylender. One owed him five hundred denarii, and the other fifty. [42]Neither of them had the money to pay him back, so he canceled the debts of both. Now which of them will love him more?"

[43]Simon replied, "I suppose the one who had the bigger debt canceled."

"You have judged correctly," Jesus said.

[44]Then he turned toward the woman and said to Simon, "Do you see this woman? I came into your house. You did not give me any water for my feet, but she wet my feet with her tears and wiped them with her hair. [45]You did not give me a kiss, but this woman, from the time I entered, has not stopped kissing my feet. [46]You did not put oil on my head, but she has poured perfume on my feet. [47]Therefore, I tell you, her many sins have been forgiven—for she loved much. But he who has been forgiven little loves little."

[48]Then Jesus said to her, "Your sins are forgiven."

⁴⁹The other guests began to say among themselves, "Who is this who even forgives sins?"
⁵⁰Jesus said to the woman, "Your faith has saved you; go in peace."

8. What is your initial impression of the woman's response to Jesus?

Does her action make you feel uncomfortable? Why or why not?

9. If you had been a guest in Simon's home and knew this woman's sinful reputation, what question would you have had about Jesus?

10. How does Jesus invite Simon to reconsider his understanding of this woman?

11. What does Jesus say to the woman, and how do the guests respond?

12. Look again at Jesus' responses to the widow, John the Baptist, Simon and the woman who anoints him. How does he uniquely minister to each one?

Which of his responses brings you hope today? Why?

■ GOING FURTHER

Take time this week to journal further about a couple of the questions above, perhaps 4 and 12.

Additional Reading

Graham Twelftree's *Jesus the Miracle Worker: A Historical and Theological Study* (Downers Grove, Ill.: InterVarsity Press, 1999) presents a detailed analysis of Jesus' many miracles and his own understanding of their purpose.

JOHN 10:14-40

The evidence from the time of Jesus is not completely clear on what constituted grounds for "blasphemy," but the evidence is clear for some of Jesus' opponents that Jesus did it. One theme unites this evidence: Jesus' claims to be able to do things normally capable only for God. Jesus may not be explicitly claiming to be God, but he is claiming to be more than the normal human.

■ OPEN

Consider your best friend from childhood or another close friend now, perhaps someone you take road trips with or sit with for hours over coffee. If you were asked to paint a picture of this relationship, what image comes to mind? Why?

■ STUDY

The apostle John was a disciple of Jesus and probably his dearest friend. Perhaps this is why he is the only one to make mention of Jesus' seven striking "I am" statements. Here Jesus uses word pictures to reveal not only who he is but also what knowledge of him looks like. Jesus describes this knowledge as an intimate relationship. "I am the bread of life. He who comes to me will never go hungry, and he who believes in me will never be thirsty," says Jesus in John 5:35. In John 15, he is the vine and those who entrust themselves to him are the branches, and here in John 10, he declares that he is the good shepherd. As one might expect, his statements stir curiosity as well as opposition. **Read John 10:14-40.**

[14]*"I am the good shepherd; I know my sheep and my sheep know me—* [15]*just as the Father knows me and I know the Father—and I lay down my life for the sheep.* [16]*I have other sheep that are not of this sheep pen. I must bring them also. They too will listen to my voice, and there shall be one flock and one shepherd.* [17]*The reason my Father loves me is that I lay down my life—only to take it up again.* [18]*No one takes it from me, but I lay it down of my own accord. I have authority to lay it down and authority to take it up again. This command I received from my Father."*

[19]*At these words the Jews were again divided.* [20]*Many of them said, "He is demon-possessed and raving mad. Why listen to him?"*

[21]*But others said, "These are not the sayings of a man possessed by a demon. Can a demon open the eyes of the blind?"*

[22]*Then came the Feast of Dedication at Jerusalem. It was winter,* [23]*and Jesus was in the temple area walking in Solomon's Colonnade.* [24]*The Jews gathered around him, saying, "How long will you keep us in suspense? If you are the Christ, tell us plainly."*

[25]*Jesus answered, "I did tell you, but you do not believe. The miracles I do in my Father's name speak for me,* [26]*but you do not believe because you are not my sheep.* [27]*My sheep listen to my voice; I know them, and they follow me.* [28]*I give them eternal life, and they shall never perish; no one can snatch them out of my hand.* [29]*My Father, who has given them to me, is greater than all; no one can snatch them out of my Father's hand.* [30]*I and the Father are one."*

³¹*Again the Jews picked up stones to stone him,* ³²*but Jesus said to them, "I have shown you many great miracles from the Father. For which of these do you stone me?"*

³³*"We are not stoning you for any of these," replied the Jews, "but for blasphemy, because you, a mere man, claim to be God."*

³⁴*Jesus answered them, "Is it not written in your Law, 'I have said you are gods'?* ³⁵*If he called them 'gods,' to whom the word of God came—and the Scripture cannot be broken—*³⁶*what about the one whom the Father set apart as his very own and sent into the world? Why then do you accuse me of blasphemy because I said, 'I am God's Son'?* ³⁷*Do not believe me unless I do what my Father does.* ³⁸*But if I do it, even though you do not believe me, believe the miracles, that you may know and understand that the Father is in me, and I in the Father."* ³⁹*Again they tried to seize him, but he escaped their grasp.*

⁴⁰*Then Jesus went back across the Jordan to the place where John had been baptizing in the early days. Here he stayed* ⁴¹*and many people came to him. They said, "Though John never performed a miraculous sign, all that John said about this man was true."* ⁴²*And in that place many believed in Jesus.*

1. What metaphor or word picture does Jesus present in this passage?

What does this picture tell us about Jesus, God and those who know him?

2. "The reason my Father loves me is that I lay down my life,"
says Jesus (verse 17). What is your first response to his words?

3. Read verses 14-16 as well as the second half of verse 17. What
context do they offer for Jesus' words in the first part of verse
17?

4. What do verses 17 and 18 reveal about Jesus' authority?
About his relationship with his Father?

It is an irony of history that *opponents sometimes confess, indi-
rectly, the truth about someone else's character, motives and mission.* This happens with the opponents of Jesus.

First, who are they? We should be very careful to avoid the
all-too-common Christian tendency to sanitize our faith by
fouling the linens of Jewish people. We tend especially to
blame the Pharisees for all things bad in Judaism. They, so we
often have said, were religious bigots who loved the externals
of worship and the showmanship of ethics; they liked fame
and avoided being merciful and just. They seem, to Christians,
to be like farces who have wandered off a local stage.

This is a false generalization—and, what is more, it is anti-
Semitism to think that one race has market control of hypoc-
risies. Should we speak of modern Christians? of the Crusad-
ers? of modern televangelists? of modern Christian parents?
We should observe two features of the Pharisees: (a) they
were good, God-fearing, law-abiding Jews, and (b) they
sometimes got themselves trapped into religious externals
and led others into their same traps. This was not because
they were Pharisees, but because they were *typical humans,*

prone to selfishness and aggrandizement!

So, no, the opponents of Jesus are not to be restricted to the Pharisees. The opponents vary from scene to scene, but the Gospel records lay especial blame on Jewish leadership. Again, not because they are Jews, but because they were threatened by Jesus in some senses and, in others, because they were doing their job.

5. How would you characterize Jesus' opponents?

In what ways were they particularly unlikeable? In what ways were they simply ordinary people trying to make sense of an extraordinary person?

6. Have you ever called someone a hypocrite or been characterized as one yourself? Why do you think this label comes so easily for most people?

7. Observe the Jewish leadership's response to Jesus in verses 19-21. Given what they witnessed and just heard, why do you think they were still conflicted?

8. Notice both the question and command posed to Jesus in verse 24. What do they reveal about the ones posing them?

9. What do you make of Jesus' answer, "I did tell you, but you
do not believe," and his subsequent response?

How does Jesus uncover his questioners' perceptions of God's
Messiah?

> In later Judaism, "blasphemy" required the use of the divine
> name (e.g., "Yahweh" or "Jehovah"), and it was a capital
> crime. But this is almost certainly not the case here; instead,
> the term is used more generically for claims of an exalted na-
> ture, claims outside the parameters of Jesus' opponents' per-
> ception of acceptable language and self-perceptions.
>
> Jesus' opponents see him transgressing those parameters
> in claiming to forgive sins (not as a *mediator* but as the
> *source!*), in accepting too much praise, for claiming to be/
> become the Son of Man before the Ancient of Days (using the
> lofty language of Daniel 7), and for his claim to be God's Son.
> Again, the desired result of the opponents may drive the
> charge and accusation: blasphemers were to be stoned to
> death (Leviticus 24:10-23). What would be surprising would
> be if Jesus' contemporaries *didn't* raise the issue of blas-
> phemy.

10. What leads Jesus' opponents to accuse him of blasphemy?
Note particularly the comments in verses 31, 33 and 36. Who
does Jesus claim to be?

11. Jesus encourages his critics to evaluate whether he is indeed who he claims to be based upon two tests. How might you also evaluate his claims?

■ GOING FURTHER

Given our study thus far, is there one question about Jesus you would like answered? Research another passage in the Bible that could provide further information, seeking assistance where needed.

Additional Reading

Take time this week, ideally in one or two sittings, to read all of Jesus' "I am" statements. See John 6:25-71; John 9—11; 14:1-14; and 15:1-17. Pay careful attention to Jesus' words about himself, his relationship with God and his promises to those who come to him. Again, how does Jesus challenge some of your expectations in these areas?

4 | Neutralizing Jesus

In his book *Can Man Live Without God?* Ravi Zacharias has this to say: "Truthfulness in the heart, said Jesus, precedes truth in the objective realm. *Intent is prior to content.* The most provocative statement Jesus made during that penetrating conversation with Pilate was that the truthfulness or falsity of an individual's heart was revealed by that person's response to Him."

■ OPEN

Recall an instance when someone spoke the truth to you and you didn't want to hear it. How did you respond? What did you learn from this experience?

■ STUDY

In his last days on earth, Jesus is betrayed by his disciple Judas, arrested and brought to the high priests Annas and Caiaphas. He is then taken to stand before the Roman governor, Pilate, who had the authority to sentence a criminal to death—which, John makes clear throughout his Gospel, was the goal of his opponents. Jesus' teaching and miracles challenge the religious leadership's authority and expectations, and now before political powers, he unnerves the pragmatic Pilate. Jesus does not mince his words, summing up his ministry in one striking remark: "Everyone on the side of truth listens to me." **Read John 18:28-40.**

[28]*Then the Jews led Jesus from Caiaphas to the palace of the Roman governor. By now it was early morning, and to avoid ceremonial uncleanness the Jews did not enter the palace; they wanted to be able to eat the Passover.* [29]*So Pilate came out to them and asked, "What charges are you bringing against this man?"*

[30]*"If he were not a criminal," they replied, "we would not have handed him over to you."*

[31]*Pilate said, "Take him yourselves and judge him by your own law."*

"But we have no right to execute anyone," the Jews objected. [32]*This happened so that the words Jesus had spoken indicating the kind of death he was going to die would be fulfilled.*

[33]*Pilate then went back inside the palace, summoned Jesus and asked him, "Are you the king of the Jews?"*

[34]*"Is that your own idea," Jesus asked, "or did others talk to you about me?"* [35]*"Am I a Jew?" Pilate replied. "It was your people and your chief priests who handed you over to me. What is it you have done?"*

[36]*Jesus said, "My kingdom is not of this world. If it were, my servants would fight to prevent my arrest by the Jews. But now my kingdom is from another place."*

[37]*"You are a king, then!" said Pilate. Jesus answered, "You are right in saying I am a king. In fact, for this reason I was born, and for this I came into the world, to testify to the truth. Everyone on the side of truth listens to me."*

[38]*"What is truth?" Pilate asked. With this he went out again to the Jews and said, "I find no basis for a charge against him.* [39]*But it is your custom for me to release to you one prisoner at the time of the Passover.*

Do you want me to release 'the king of the Jews'?"
⁴⁰*They shouted back, "No, not him! Give us Barabbas!" Now Barabbas had taken part in a rebellion.*

1. Imagine you are outside the palace witnessing the exchange between the Jewish leadership and this Roman governor. Describe what you see, hear and feel.

2. Pilate tells those who have brought Jesus to him, "Take him yourselves and judge him by your own law" (verse 31). What does their reply tell us about their ultimate intentions?

3. Notice John's remark in verse 32. What is your initial response to these words?

What we have sketched here is a *Christology of opposition,* a Christology (that is, a theological understanding of the person and work of Christ) based on what we know about Jesus as a result of charges laid against him by his opponents. What does impress us is the thread—and threat!—of stoning that runs through several of the charges, and this thread runs into a cross rather than a stoning. This suggests quite convincingly that the charges were not made up, for *had the early Christians made them up they would be attributing to Jesus expectations that did not come about.* It is highly likely that Jesus *expected* a death, expressed at times as a stoning, but the strange twist of events at the end of his life led instead to a Cross. The impact of these charges is simple: Jesus was perceived as a prophet who had a significant impact on people around him, in Galilee and Judea, and the opponents thought he was leading people astray, in practice and ideas. He should be seen as a rebellious son and lawbreaker who, through magic and demon-inspiration, was able to perform mighty deeds. But the clincher in all of this is that he made claims about himself that transgress Jewish sensibilities about God.

4. How do the charges and threats made against Jesus contribute to our understanding of Jesus?

5. Verse 33 transitions us from Pilate's exchange with the religious authorities to his conversation with Jesus. What is his first question to Jesus? Why do you think he asks this?

6. Why did Jesus respond to Pilate's question the way that he did (verse 34)?

How does the meaning of Pilate's question change if he personally wants to know Jesus' identity, as opposed to verifying the authorities' accusation?

Let us see, now, how Jesus approached Pilate's question. The conversation had begun with Pilate asking Jesus if, indeed, He was a king. The very surprising answer of Jesus was, "Is that your idea, or did others talk to you about me?" (John 18:34).

This is the first and most important step to understanding the nature of truth. In effect, Jesus was asking Pilate if this was a genuine question or purely an academic one. He was not merely checking on Pilate's sincerity. He was opening up Pilate's heart to himself to reveal to Pilate his unwillingness to deal with the implications of Jesus' answer. Intent in the pursuit of truth is prior to content, or to the availability of it. Author George MacDonald once said, "To give truth to him who loves it not is only to give him more plentiful reasons for misinterpretation." The love of truth and the willingness to submit to its demands is the first step.

But Jesus said something else that is even more extraordinary. After identifying His Lordship in a kingdom that was not of this world, He said, "Everyone on the side of truth *listens to me*" (John 18:37, italics mine). Jesus was not merely establishing the existence of truth but His pristine embodiment of it. He was *identical* to the truth. This meant that everything He said and did, and the life He lived in the flesh, represented that which was in keeping with ultimate reality. Therefore, to reject Him is to choose to govern oneself with a lie.[2]

7. Comment on the assertion that "intent in the pursuit of truth is prior to content, or to the availability of it." Do you agree or disagree? Why?

---

[2]Ravi Zacharias, *Deliver Us from Evil* (Dallas: Word Publishing, 1996), p. 222.

8. What do you think it means that "everything [Jesus] said and did, and the life He lived in the flesh, represented that which was in keeping with ultimate reality"?

9. Jesus states unequivocally to Pilate, "Everyone on the side of truth listens to me." What does Pilate intend to accomplish by his reply? Does he succeed?

10. What does it take for you to stay "on the side of truth" in your everyday life?

■ GOING FURTHER

Explore one or two questions in this chapter further. Perhaps some agitated or confused you. Why do you think this may be? Jesus said, "I came into the world, to testify to the truth." Consider asking God to show you the truth as you work through your questions.

Additional Reading

Ravi Zacharias examines Jesus' interaction with Pilate as well as the striking difference between Jesus' response and other religious prophets in his chapter "When God Was Silent" in his book *Jesus Among Other Gods* (Nashville: Word, 2000), pp. 141-64.

LUKE 6:43—7:10

In *Jesus Among Other Gods* Ravi Zacharias asserts that faith, defined biblically, "is not antithetical to reason. It is not just a will to believe, everything to the contrary notwithstanding. . . . Faith in the biblical sense is substantive, based on the knowledge that the One in whom that faith is placed has proven that He is worthy of that trust. In its essence, *faith is a confidence in the person of Jesus Christ and in His power, so that even when His power does not serve my end, my confidence in Him remains because of who He is.*"

■ OPEN

Think of some people you highly trust. What is it that makes them especially trustworthy?

■ STUDY

Luke is the only Gospel writer to record Jesus' Sermon on the Plain, a shorter version of his Sermon on the Mount. The disciple writes, "Jesus went out to a mountainside to pray, and spent the night praying to God. When morning came, he called his disciples to him and chose twelve of them, whom he also designated apostles" (Luke 6:12-13). Jesus then addresses a crowd "who had come to hear him and to be healed of their diseases" (verse 18). As we saw earlier, here again he preaches with word pictures of those who profess him to be Lord. Afterward Jesus goes to Capernaum where he learns of a man in great need. This passage comes immediately before the raising of the widow's dead son that we examined in study two. **Read Luke 6:43—7:10.**

⁴³*"No good tree bears bad fruit, nor does a bad tree bear good fruit.* ⁴⁴*Each tree is recognized by its own fruit. People do not pick figs from thornbushes, or grapes from briers.* ⁴⁵*The good man brings good things out of the good stored up in his heart, and the evil man brings evil things out of the evil stored up in his heart. For out of the overflow of his heart his mouth speaks.*

⁴⁶*Why do you call me, 'Lord, Lord,' and do not do what I say?* ⁴⁷*I will show you what he is like who comes to me and hears my words and puts them into practice.* ⁴⁸*He is like a man building a house, who dug down deep and laid the foundation on rock. When a flood came, the torrent struck that house but could not shake it, because it was well built.* ⁴⁹*But the one who hears my words and does not put them into practice is like a man who built a house on the ground without a foundation. The moment the torrent struck that house, it collapsed and its destruction was complete."*

⁷:¹*When Jesus had finished saying all this in the hearing of the people, he entered Capernaum.* ²*There a centurion's servant, whom his master valued highly, was sick and about to die.* ³*The centurion heard of Jesus and sent some elders of the Jews to him, asking him to come and heal his servant.* ⁴*When they came to Jesus, they pleaded earnestly with him, "This man deserves to have you do this,* ⁵*because he loves our nation and has built our synagogue."* ⁶*So Jesus went with them.*

He was not far from the house when the centurion sent friends to say to him: "Lord, don't trouble yourself, for I do not deserve to have

you come under my roof. ⁷*That is why I did not even consider myself
worthy to come to you. But say the word, and my servant will be
healed.* ⁸*For I myself am a man under authority, with soldiers under
me. I tell this one, 'Go,' and he goes; and that one, 'Come,' and he
comes. I say to my servant, 'Do this,' and he does it."*

⁹*When Jesus heard this, he was amazed at him, and turning to the
crowd following him, he said, "I tell you, I have not found such great
faith even in Israel."* ¹⁰*Then the men who had been sent returned to
the house and found the servant well.*

1. What comparisons does Jesus make in verses 43-45? What is
his point?

2. Reflect on the proverb "out of the overflow of his heart his
mouth speaks." What examples come to mind of this happen-
ing?

3. If you had been in the crowd, what might you be feeling and
thinking upon hearing Jesus say (in verse 46), "Why do you
call me, 'Lord, Lord,' and do not do what I say?" Why?

The phrase "my Lord" was common in Judaism at the time of
Jesus, and the evidence of the Gospels suggests that Jesus was
addressed by his followers at times with the label "Lord."
More importantly the term *Lord* emerges from a *relationship*

> with Jesus, which is as much one of *miracle-working power* as it is of *teaching* and *ruling on legal issues*. It is difficult for us now to think our way back into the minds of Jesus' followers to see just how much exaltedness is latent in the term **Lord**. I find it possible that with this term the disciples labeled Jesus with a title that revealed that they thought Jesus was more than a prophet and more than a typical teacher.

4. People ascribed to Jesus the title *Lord* for a number of reasons. What are some of them?

5. What does the use of the term *Lord* by Jesus' followers suggest about how people understood Jesus?

6. How does Jesus characterize the person who "hears my words and puts them into practice" and the one who does not do this?

When do you find this easier to do? When is this more difficult?

7. Why do you think the centurion evoked such amazement in Jesus?

One of the most startling things about life is that it does not start with reason and end with faith. It starts in childhood with faith and is sustained either by reasoning through that faith or by blindly leaving the reason for faith unaddressed. The child's mind has a very limited capacity to inform it of the reason for its trust. But whether she nestles on her mother's shoulder, nurses at her mother's breast, or runs into her father's arms, she does so because of an implicit trust that those shoulders will bear her, that her food will sustain her, and that those arms will hold her. If over time that trust is tested, it will be the character of the parent that will either prove that trust wise or foolish. Faith is not bereft of reason. . . .

Faith in Jesus Christ is a cognitive, passionate, and moral commitment to that which stands up under the scrutiny of the mind, the heart, and the conscience. It is not an escapist grasp that comes to the rescue when life is out of control. It is recasting every threat and possibility that life presents into the design of God.[3]

8. According to the above passage, what does biblical faith look like?

9. How would you characterize the ability to trust others, and especially God?

Does it come easily or must it be continually earned? Why do you think this might be?

[3]Ravi Zacharias, *Jesus Among Other Gods* (Nashville: Word Publishing, 2000), pp. 58, 60, 66.

10. Jesus reveals that true faith in God—like a growing relationship—is "dug down deep" in order to lay "the foundation on rock" (verse 48). It involves putting into practice one's commitments, humility and trust, such that faith is able to stand through life's storms. What step(s) might you take this week to build a solid foundation?

What encouragement do you take from Jesus' words?

■ GOING FURTHER

How would you measure your faith in God right now? Are you having trouble putting faith into practice, or are you like the centurion, taking him at his word? Is your knowledge of God distant and fearful or intimate and trusting? Ask God to help you dig deep to reveal how you might build a solid foundation upon him.

Additional Reading

Pastor and scholar John R. W. Stott examines what it means to follow Christ in his readable and informative book *Basic Christianity* (Downers Grove, Ill.: InterVarsity Press, 2007). See especially "Part Four: Man's Response."

MATTHEW 6:25-34; 7:7-12

The Sermon the Mount has to be understood as Matthew's presentation of who Jesus is, what he teaches, and what he calls people to be and to do. This is not secondary teaching for the fully committed after they have chosen to "accept" Jesus, but it is what must be understood as the very summons of Jesus himself. In other words, this is Jesus' evangelistic summons.

■ OPEN

Which of the following phrases most consistently describes you: "I am somewhat anxious" or "I am pretty carefree"? Why?

■ STUDY

It is difficult to walk away from Jesus' teaching on the Sermon on the Mount without some emotion or questions, for his words are direct and even radical. Bible scholar R. T. France concludes, "The Sermon . . . presents the radical demand of Jesus the Messiah on all who would respond to his preaching of God's kingdom." *Read Matthew 6:25-34; 7:7-12.*

²⁵*"Therefore I tell you, do not worry about your life, what you will eat or drink; or about your body, what you will wear. Is not life more im-*

portant than food, and the body more important than clothes? ^{26}*Look at the birds of the air; they do not sow or reap or store away in barns, and yet your heavenly Father feeds them. Are you not much more valuable than they?* ^{27}*Who of you by worrying can add a single hour to his life?*

^{28}*And why do you worry about clothes? See how the lilies of the field grow. They do not labor or spin.* ^{29}*Yet I tell you that not even Solomon in all his splendor was dressed like one of these.* ^{30}*If that is how God clothes the grass of the field, which is here today and tomorrow is thrown into the fire, will he not much more clothe you, O you of little faith?* ^{31}*So do not worry, saying, 'What shall we eat?' or 'What shall we drink?' or 'What shall we wear?'* ^{32}*For the pagans run after all these things, and your heavenly Father knows that you need them.* ^{33}*But seek first his kingdom and his righteousness, and all these things will be given to you as well.* ^{34}*Therefore do not worry about tomorrow, for tomorrow will worry about itself. Each day has enough trouble of its own."*

$^{7:7}$*"Ask and it will be given to you; seek and you will find; knock and the door will be opened to you.* ^{8}*For everyone who asks receives; he who seeks finds; and to him who knocks, the door will be opened.*

^{9}*Which of you, if his son asks for bread, will give him a stone?* ^{10}*Or if he asks for a fish, will give him a snake?* ^{11}*If you, then, though you are evil, know how to give good gifts to your children, how much more will your Father in heaven give good gifts to those who ask him!* ^{12}*So in everything, do to others what you would have them do to you, for this sums up the Law and the Prophets."*

1. Notice the three commands that Jesus gives in verses 25-28. How would you summarize his instruction?

2. Twice Jesus invites us to understand God as "heavenly father" (see verses 26, 32). What positive emotions might thinking of God as Father elicit in people? What negative emotions? How do you think Jesus intended it to be understood?

3. Jesus portrays his listeners as having "little faith" (verse 30). Why do you think he says this?

4. Three times in this brief passage Jesus says, "Do not worry." When are you most likely to worry and to disbelieve God?

The Sermon on the Mount is a summary of Jesus' teaching and preaching, which means it is where one goes to hear what Jesus taught and what he preached if one wants to make up her or his mind about following Jesus.

Here is a consummate evangelistic invitation: "Now that you've heard what I believe in and what I am summoning you to be and do," I hear Jesus saying, "let me summon you to follow along." The whole Sermon on the Mount comes down to being foolish or wise. The foolish person hears the words of Jesus and fails to practice them; the wise person hears the words of Jesus and practices them.

The Sermon on the Mount is more than the ethics that follow conversion: the Sermon on the Mount is the summons of
Jesus himself for those who want to follow him. This is not
second-layer stuff but entry stuff; this is not a lesson in ethics but a radical summons to surrender. Indeed, it is ethics
and discipleship, but that is because one cannot have conversion or following Jesus without ethics and discipleship.

5. According to the passage above, how should we understand
the Sermon on the Mount?

6. In what ways do you see Jesus' teaching here as "not a lesson
in ethics but a radical summons to surrender"?

7. Look again at verses 32-33. What comparison does Jesus
make? What do you think he means by this instruction?

Frankly, the sort of things that you can know with absolute
certainty are actually not that important. . . .
    The beliefs which are really important in life concern such
things as whether there is a God and what he is like, or the
mystery of human nature and destiny. . . . In the first place,
they are *relevant* to life. They matter, in that they affect the
way in which we think, live, hope and act. In the second
place, they *cannot be proved* (or disproved) with total certainty. By their very nature, they make claims that cannot be

proved with certainty. At best, we may hope to know them as
probably true. There will always be an element of doubt in
any statement which goes beyond the world of logic and self-
evident propositions. Christianity shares this situation. It is
not unique in this respect: an atheist or Marxist is confronted
with precisely the same dilemma. . . .
    There is indeed a leap of faith involved in Christianity—
but it is not an irrational leap into the dark. The Christian experience is that of being caught safely by a loving and living
God, whose arms await us as we leap. Martin Luther put this
rather well: "Faith is a free surrender and a joyous wager on
the unseen, untried and unknown goodness of God."[4]

8. What does the idea that "the sort of things that you can know
   with absolute certainty are actually not that important" tell us
   about how we arrive at knowing God and anything worth
   knowing?

9. Restate Martin Luther's definition of faith in your own words.
   Do you find this a gratifying or troubling characterization?
   Why?

10. Read again Matthew 7:7-12. In contrast to worry, what does
    Jesus instruct us to do (see verses 7-8)?

[4]Alister McGrath, *Doubting* (Downers Grove, Ill.: InterVarsity Press, 2007).

How does this instruction relate to Matthew 6:33?

11. Jesus encourages us to surrender ourselves to a loving relationship with our heavenly Father who knows what we need. How has your relationship with Jesus and God the Father changed during the course of this study?

■ GOING FURTHER

In this booklet we have examined what it means to follow Jesus—that is, to surrender our hopes and very lives to him. If Jesus asked you today, "Do you know me and will you follow me?" how would you answer beyond a simple "yes" or "no"? Take time to journal, talk to someone, and pray about your response.

Additional Reading

In his chapter "Sons of God," theologian J. I. Packer begins, "What is a Christian? . . . The richest answer I know is that a Christian is one who has God for his Father." Here in his classic book *Knowing God* (Downers Grove, Ill.: InterVarsity Press, 1993), he addresses the significance of God adopting Jesus' followers into his family.

Leader's Notes

Leading a small group discussion can be an enjoyable and rewarding experience. But it can also be *scary*—especially if you've never done it before. If this is your feeling, you're in good company. When God asked Moses to lead the Israelites out of Egypt, he replied, "O LORD, please send someone else to do it" (Ex 4:13). It was the same with Solomon, Jeremiah and Timothy, but God helped these people in spite of their weaknesses, and he will help you as well.

You don't need to be an expert on the Bible or a trained teacher to lead a group discussion. The idea behind these studies is that the leader guides group members in their exploration of critical questions in the life of faith. This method of learning will allow group members to remember much more of what is said than a lecture would.

These studies are designed to be led easily. As a matter of fact, the flow of questions is so natural that you may feel that the studies lead themselves. This study guide is also flexible. You can use it with a variety of groups—student, professional, neighborhood or church groups. Each study takes around sixty minutes in a group setting.

There are some important facts to know about group dynamics and encouraging discussion. The suggestions listed below should enable you to effectively and enjoyably fulfill your role as leader.

■ PREPARING FOR THE STUDY

1. Ask God to help you understand and apply the material in each session for your own life. Unless this happens, you will not be prepared to lead others. Pray too for the various members of the group. Ask God to open your hearts to the message of his Word and motivate you to action.

2. Read the introduction to the entire guide to get an overview of the entire book and the issues which will be explored.

3. As you begin each study, read and reread the assigned material to familiarize yourself with it.

4. Carefully work through each question in the study. Spend time in meditation and reflection as you consider how to respond.

5. Write your thoughts and responses in the space provided in the study guide. This will help you to express your understanding of the material clearly.

6. It might help to have a Bible dictionary handy. Use it to look up any unfamiliar words, names or places. (For additional help on how to study a passage, see chapter five of *How to Lead a LifeGuide Bible Study,* InterVarsity Press.)

7. Consider how the Scripture applies to your life. Remember that the group will follow your lead in responding to the studies. They will not go any deeper than you do.

8. Once you have finished your own study of the passage, familiarize yourself with the leader's notes for the study you are leading. These are designed to help you in several ways. First, they tell you the purpose the study guide author had in mind when writing the study. Take time to think through how the study questions work together to accomplish that purpose. Second, the notes provide you with additional background information for various questions. This infor-

mation can be useful when people have difficulty understanding or answering a question. Third, the leader's notes can alert you to potential problems you may encounter during the study.

9. If you wish to remind yourself of anything mentioned in the leader's notes, make a note to yourself below that question in the study.

■ LEADING THE STUDY

1. Begin the study on time. Open with prayer, asking God to help the group to understand and apply the material being discussed.

2. Be sure that everyone in your group has a study guide. Encourage the group to prepare beforehand for each discussion by reading the introduction to the guide and by working through the questions in that week's session.

3. At the beginning of your first time together, explain that these studies are meant to be discussions, not lectures. Encourage the members of the group to participate. However, do not put pressure on those who may be hesitant to speak during the first few sessions. You may want to suggest the following guidelines to your group.

• Stick to the topic being discussed.

• Your responses should be based on the material provided and not on outside authorities such as commentaries or speakers.

• Only rarely should you refer to other portions of the Bible. This allows for everyone to participate in in-depth study on equal ground.

• Anything said in the group is considered confidential and will not be discussed outside the group unless specific permission is given to do so.

• We will listen attentively to each other and provide time for each person present to talk.

• We will pray for each other.

4. Have a group member read the introduction at the beginning of the discussion.

5. Every session begins with a group discussion question. The question or activity is meant to be used before the passage is read. The question introduces the theme of the study and encourages group members to begin to open up. Encourage as many members as possible to participate, and be ready to get the discussion going with your own response.

This section is designed to reveal where our thoughts or feelings need to be transformed by the renewing of our minds. That is why it is especially important not to read the passage to the group members before the discussion question is asked. The passage will tend to color the honest reactions people would otherwise give because they are, of course, supposed to think the way the Bible does.

You may want to supplement the group discussion question with an icebreaker to help people to get comfortable. See the community section of *Small Group Idea Book* for more ideas.

6. Have a group member (or members if the passage is long) read aloud the textual material as it occurs in the session. Then give people several minutes to read the passage again silently so that they can take it all in.

7. As you ask the questions, keep in mind that they are designed to be used just as they are written. You may simply read them aloud. Or you may prefer to express them in your own words. There may be times when it is appropriate to deviate from the study guide. For example, a question may have already been answered. If so, move on to the next question. Or someone may raise an important question not covered in the guide. Take time to discuss it, but try to keep the group from going off on tangents.

8. Avoid answering your own questions. If necessary, repeat or rephrase them until they are clearly understood. Or point out something you read in the leader's notes to clarify the context or meaning. An eager group quickly becomes passive and silent if they think the leader will do most of the talking.

9. Don't be afraid of silence. People may need time to think about the question before formulating their answers.

10. Don't be content with just one answer. Ask, "What do the rest of you think?" or "Anything else?" until several people have given answers to the question.

11. Acknowledge all contributions. Try to be affirming whenever possible. Never reject an answer. If it is clearly off-base, ask, "Which verse led you to that conclusion?" or again, "What do the rest of you think?"

12. Don't expect every answer to be addressed to you, even though this will probably happen at first. As group members become more at ease, they will begin to truly interact with each other. This is one sign of healthy discussion.

13. Don't be afraid of controversy. It can be very stimulating. If you don't resolve an issue completely, don't be frustrated. Move on and keep it in mind for later. A subsequent study may solve the problem.

14. Periodically summarize what the group has said to that point. This helps to draw together the various ideas mentioned and gives continuity to the discussion. But don't preach.

15. Give an opportunity during the session for people to talk about what they are learning.

16. Conclude your time together with conversational prayer. Ask for

God's help in working through the implications of the discussion.

17. End on time.

■ COMPONENTS OF SMALL GROUPS

A healthy small group should do more than study the Bible. There are four components to consider as you structure your time together.

- *Nurture.* Small groups help us to grow in our knowledge and love of God. Bible study is the key to making this happen and is the foundation of your small group.

- *Community.* Small groups are a great place to develop deep friendships with other Christians. Allow time for informal interaction before and after each discussion. Plan activities and games that will help you get to know each other. Spend time having fun together—going on a picnic or cooking dinner together.

- *Worship and prayer.* Your study will be enhanced by spending time praising God together in prayer or song. Pray for each other's needs—and keep track of how God is answering prayer in your group. Ask God to help you to apply what you are learning in your study.

- *Outreach.* Reaching out to others can be a practical way of applying what you are learning, and it will keep your group from becoming self-focused. Host a series of evangelistic discussions for your friends or neighbors. Clean up the yard of an elderly friend. Serve at a soup kitchen together, or spend a day working on a Habitat house.

Many more suggestions and helps in each of these areas are found in *Small Group Idea Book.* Information on building a small group can be found in *Small Group Leaders' Handbook* and *The Big Book on Small Groups* (both from InterVarsity Press). Reading through one of these books would be worth your time.

STUDY 1

Meeting Jesus

MARK 2:1-12

Purpose: **To show that Jesus elicited amazement in the various crowds who encountered him.**

QUESTION 1. When the people hear that Jesus has come home to Capernaum (the region in Galilee that became his home after leaving Nazareth), they gather to meet him. Mark introduces us to Jesus in his opening chapter through several fast-paced clips: After his baptism and temptation, "Jesus went into Galilee, proclaiming the good news of God. 'The time has come,' he said. 'The kingdom of God is near. Repent and believe the good news!'" (Mk 1:14-15). Jesus' calling of his disciples elicits an *immediate* response (see 1:18, 20). In fact, Mark uses this construction "and immediately" (*kai euthus*) eight more times in this chapter alone (vv. 10, 12, 21, 23, 28, 29, 30, 42), showing that Jesus' authoritative words and healings commanded instant attention.

QUESTIONS 2-3. Whereas the crowds who gathered saw a strange commotion on the roof above them, Jesus saw "their faith"—the faith of the paralytic and his four friends who believed Jesus could heal him. That is, Jesus sees the *intentions of the heart,* as evidenced again in verse 8: "Immediately Jesus knew in his spirit that this was what they were thinking in their hearts, and he said to them, 'Why are you thinking these things?'" So Jesus' direct response goes (if you will) right to the heart: "Son, your sins are forgiven" (v. 5). In saying this, Jesus reveals the true purpose of his ministry: to restore broken people to God. Yes, we are broken by the frailties of our humanness—sickness, injury, rejection—but ultimately our souls bear the marks of our sin and alienation from God. Thus it is noteworthy that the first words we hear from Jesus' lips in this Gospel are "The time has come. The kingdom of God is near.

Repent and believe the good news!" (1:15). Moreover, by calling the paralytic "son," Jesus confirms that he is now a son of his heavenly Father—his faith has indeed made him whole.

QUESTIONS 4-5. It makes little sense to assume that the crowd in one location is the same as in another. Since I was a youngster daydreaming during sermons, paying attention here and there, and especially to the illustrations, I have heard that the crowds who loved Jesus when he entered into Jerusalem (Mt 21), in some cruel joke turned against him when he was on trial and let him go to the cross. But *there is no reason to think the two crowds are the same.* Perhaps some of those at the entry into Jerusalem hung around long enough to turn against him, but we have no knowledge of such a conversion (or apostasy), and in the absence of such information, we are best leaving the term "crowd" to be what it is—an odd collection of people.

The various crowds are amazed at Jesus' words and healings and report to others what they witnessed. Moreover, because their statements were not doctrinal claims (such as Peter's confession "you are the Christ" in Mark 8:29) but expressions of sheer amazement, we are on firm grounds to believe what they observed was in keeping with what took place. Indeed, it is quite striking to compare the response of the crowd and teachers of the law in the scene with the paralytic to that of an unclean spirit in Mark 1:23-26. Upon healing the paralytic everyone exclaimed, "We have never seen anything like this" (2:12); they recognize Jesus' authority and uniqueness. And yet, throughout the Gospels we find that demonic powers immediately recognize something more: they are in *the very presence of God.* Before Jesus casts him out, the unclean spirit in the man in Mark 1:24 cries out, "I know who you are—the Holy One of God."

QUESTION 7. The teachers of the law are upset when Jesus declares that he has forgiven the paralytic of his sins, for only God can do such a thing. The evidence from the time of Jesus is not completely clear on what constituted grounds for "blasphemy," but the evidence is clear for some of Jesus' opponents that Jesus did it.

One theme unites this evidence: Jesus' claims to be able to do things normally capable only for God. In essence, there is a claim here of an exalted status, whether now or in the future. In later Judaism, "blasphemy" required the use of the divine name (e.g., YHWH [or Yahweh/Jehovah]), and it was a capital crime. But this is almost certainly not the case here.

New Testament scholar Craig Keener adds, "Judaism taught that only God could forgive sins, but most Jews allowed that some of God's representatives could speak on God's behalf. The passive form, 'are forgiven,' could be interpreted in this way (Jewish teachers often used the passive form to describe God's activity); but Jesus was not a priest, no one had offered sacrifice, and the scribes [teachers of the law] had heard no basis for the pronouncement of forgiveness, not even clear indication of repentance.

"The Old Testament penalty for blaspheming God's name—reproaching rather than honoring it—was death (Lev 24:10–23). According to subsequent Jewish teaching, blasphemy involved pronouncing the divine name or inviting people to follow other gods. Strictly speaking, therefore, these legal scholars would have been mistaken in interpreting Jesus' words as blasphemy, even by their own rules. But the term was used much more broadly in popular parlance in this period, and they may apply it in the general sense of dishonoring the divine name" (Keener, *The IVP Bible Background Commentary: New Testament* [Downers Grove, Ill.: InterVarsity Press, 1997], p. 140).

QUESTIONS 7-8, 10. Commentator Alan Cole offers some significant insight here: "[The teachers of the law] saw at once down to the theological roots of the matter. Of course, none but God could forgive sin; how dare a mere human like Jesus claim such authority? Again and again during the life of Jesus the same dilemma was to re-appear. If He were not divine, then He was indeed a blasphemer: for He must be 'either God, or mad, or bad', as the old saying runs. There could be no other possible explanation. If the scribes did not accept Him, then they must condemn Him. At least some of them would see the logic of this (3:6) and so they would begin to plot His death in cold blood. Already the path of the cross was determined.

"Nevertheless, in the case of some of the scribes, the bewilderment may have been genuine enough, as it surely was in the case of the honest scribe of 12:34. To help such bewildered people to make the staggering equation between the human Jesus and Godhead, Jesus gave them an unmasked sign of His divine power, by healing the paralytic before their eyes.

"Of course, it was equally easy to utter the two phrases in the text, and equally easy for divine power to vindicate the note of authority in either phrase. But there is no outward sign by which the inward reality of the forgiveness of sins can be tested. . . . So, as often, Jesus took His enemies on their own terms and refuted them; verse 8 shows that He acted in full knowledge of their thought processes. It was, in point of fact, a much easier thing to heal the body than to restore the soul, for even a prophet might heal, while no mere prophet could ever forgive sins; but the scribes, with their incessant demands for visible signs, were unlikely to see this (8:11). In any case, Jesus both healed and forgave on this occasion, leaving them speechless. If they had eyes to see it, here was the very sign they had wanted; but none are so blind as those who refuse to see" (R. Alan Cole, *Mark*, Tyndale New Testament Commentaries [Downers Grove, Ill.: InterVarsity Press, 2002], pp. 120-21).

STUDY 2

Looking for Jesus
LUKE 7:11-23, 36-50

Purpose: **To show that Jesus met and challenged people's expectations of a prophet of God.**

QUESTIONS 1-2. Jesus' immediate response to the funeral he sees when he approaches town is to extend compassion to the bereaved. Luke poignantly observes, "His heart went out to her and he said, 'Don't cry' " (7:13). In this instance, the grieving is a widow who has also just lost her only son. "For a widow's only son to die before she did was considered extremely tragic; it also left her dependent on public charity for support unless she had other relatives of means," notes Craig Keener (*IVP Bible Background Commentary: New Testament*, p. 207).

Jesus further reveals his compassion for the widow by touching her son's coffin, an act that would make him ceremonially unclean but that unites him to this family. He then speaks to the dead to arise, and the young man gets up.

Darrell Bock observes, "This miracle is reminiscent of the Old Testament resuscitations performed by Elijah (1 Kings 17:17-24) and Elisha (2 Kings 4:32-37). . . . Such historical background explains why the crowds come to see Jesus as a *great prophet*. The Old Testament precedents help explain the event. Given such precedents, the reader should not jump to conclusions about what such events prove about Jesus' divinity, especially since Peter and Paul will do similar works. The belief that Jesus is divine has other bases" (Darrell Bock, *Luke,* IVP New Testament Commentary Series [Downers Grove, Ill.: InterVarsity Press, 1994], p. 135).

QUESTIONS 4-5. John the Baptist, who came to prepare the way for the Lord, is thrown into prison after rebuking Herod for taking his brother's wife (Lk 3:19-20). When he hears of Jesus performing miracles while he himself has not been released from prison, he wonders whether Jesus is indeed who he claimed to be. Notice that Luke repeats John's question twice—"Are you the one who was to come or should we expect someone else?—emphasizing the intensity of the beleaguered disciple's struggle. Jesus' compassionate reply is intended to point John to what God is doing. He affirms John's role as a forerunner of the Messiah by alluding to Isaiah's messianic prophecy: "In that day the deaf will hear the words of the scroll, and out of gloom and darkness the eyes of the blind will see" (Is 29:18). Furthermore, Jesus' statement "Blessed is the man who does not fall away on account of me" is both an encouragement to continue in faithfulness and a blessing upon John who has not fallen away. Indeed, in the verses that follow, Jesus commends John's ministry before the crowd. He is "more than a prophet. This is the one about whom it is written: 'I will send my messenger ahead of you, who will prepare your way before you' " (vv. 26-27).

Darrell Bocks adds, "The term for 'offense' [the NIV reads "does not fall away"], *skandalon,* is frequently used in this sense of reacting negatively, often with reference to Isaiah 8:14. . . . This term could refer to a trap or a stumbling block . . . to something that ensnares and prevents progress. Jesus is saying to John and others that blessing comes to the one not offended by the uniqueness of Jesus' way of ministry. The fact that Jesus' style of ministry is unexpected should not trip people up. Though stated negatively, the verse is a call to trust Jesus and recognize that he knows the way that he is going" (Bock, *Luke,* pp. 137-38).

QUESTION 8. Bible scholar Leon Morris provides a perceptive understanding of the woman's anointing of Jesus: "Each Gospel has a story of an anointing of Jesus by a woman. . . . There are good reasons for thinking that the other three are describing one and the same incident but Luke a different one. They refer to an incident in the last week of Jesus' life, Luke to one much earlier. The 'sinner' of Luke's account wet Jesus' feet with tears, wiped them with her hair, kissed and anointed them, which is different from what we read in the other accounts, as is the ensuing discussion. In Luke it is concerned with love and forgiveness, in the others in selling the unguent [ointment] and giving to the poor. . . .

"It is fair conjecture that Jesus had turned this woman from her sinful ways and that all this was the expression of her love and gratitude. It is not clear whether she had met Jesus. She may simply have been among the crowds who listened to his teaching and had been so convicted that her life had been changed" (Leon Morris, *Luke,* Tyndale New Testament Commentaries [Downers Grove, Ill.: InterVarsity Press, 1994], pp. 160-62).

QUESTIONS 10-11. Jesus knows what Simon is thinking—*If this man were a prophet*—and shrewdly counters his skepticism by telling him a parable. Throughout the Gospels Jesus uses such parables to speak forth judgment and invite repentance. "He who has ears, let him hear," declares Jesus in Matthew 11:15 (a parallel passage to Jesus' commendation of John's ministry here in Luke 7). Jesus then invites Simon to respond, and affirms his answer.

Darrell Bock writes, "[Jesus] notes that the woman has done what the Pharisee has failed to do. It is not clear that the Pharisee has actually failed to do what is culturally expected. . . . But what the woman has done goes above and beyond the call of duty. Love often produces such an extraordinary response. . . .

"If Jesus' reception of the sinner is a problem, his declaration of the forgiveness of sins is a massive problem (compare 5:22)! Only God forgives sin. Again we see how Jesus' ministry . . . is an example of how to relate to others but also reflects a unique authority that makes Jesus more than a mere instructor of morality. In saying the woman's sins are forgiven, he is clearly even greater than a prophet. Here is raw authority. . . .

"[The Pharisees] know no mere man has the right to forgive sin, so they ask, '*Who is this who even forgives sin?*' The question is crucial. If Jesus has the authority to forgive sin, then he has the right to reveal how salvation occurs. Simon was worried about Jesus being a prophet, but Jesus' pronouncement of forgiveness means he is much more" (Bock, *Luke,* p. 143).

STUDY 3
Rejecting Jesus
JOHN 10:14-40

Purpose: **To show that both Jesus' miracles and his words about God challenged the religious authorities' expectations of God's Messiah.**

QUESTION 1. Although the Old Testament and Jewish leaders acknowledged God as Father, Jesus expressed a more intimate relationship with him, especially by calling him "*my* Father." After healing a man on the Sabbath, John 5:17-18 tells us, "Jesus said to them, 'My Father is always at work to this very day, and I, too, am working.' For this reason the Jews tried all the harder to kill him; not only was he breaking the Sabbath, but he was even calling God his own Father, making himself equal with God." It is critical to note that Jesus, however, does not equate himself with God. In John 5:19-27—and in the passage from John 10—he declares his dependence on and oneness with his Father: "The Son can do nothing by himself; he can only do what he sees his Father doing, because what the Father does the Son also does" (5:19).

Bible scholar Rodney Whitacre comments, "If we want to understand who Jesus is, John says, we must begin with the relationship shared between the Father and the Son 'before the world began' (John 17:5; 24). This relationship is the central revelation of this Gospel and the key to understanding all that Jesus says and does. . . .

"Jesus' knowledge of his flock and their knowledge of him (v. 14) are compared to the knowledge the Father and the Son have of another (v. 15). . . . As always, Jesus' identity as the Son and his relationship with the Father are crucial for understanding what is being said.

"This knowledge is not simply a knowledge about one another or merely the knowledge of an acquaintance. Rather, it is an intimacy that is love. The intimacy of the Father and Son is so close it is described as a oneness (10:30), and a similar oneness of life is affirmed between Jesus and his disciples (for example, 15:1-7)" (Rodney A. Whitacre, *John*, The IVP New Testament Commentary Series [Downers Grove, Ill.: InterVarsity Press, 1999], pp. 50, 262-63).

QUESTIONS 2-4. The late theologian Lesslie Newbigin offers this wisdom: "The good shepherd knows his sheep and his sheep know him. This deep mutual knowing rests upon and is a participation in the mutual knowing which binds Jesus to the Father. . . . It is not just the 'objective' knowledge which leaves the knower uncommitted. It is a knowledge which is only present in a total self-giving, and—once again—this is rooted in the total mutual self-giving which is the life of God. The Father gives his Son for the life of the world; the Son gives back his life to the Father, and thus the glory of God is revealed in the world. . . .

"The action of Jesus in giving his life is an act both of complete freedom and of filial obedience. He is not the passive victim of other's men purposes. . . . Jesus goes forward on the path which his Father has prepared for him, and does so with obedient freedom and a free obedience. This path is that of unswerving witness to the truth, which necessarily draws upon itself the hatred of those who live by the lie. Jesus in going this way offers his life to the Father in whose will is his joy (15:11), confident that what he has so freely offered cannot be lost but will be received back. This path of freely willed and obedient surrender to the Father is the way which Jesus is, and along which he leads his people" (Newbigin, *The Light Has Come: An Exposition of the Fourth Gospel* [Grand Rapids: Eerdmans, 1982], pp. 129-30).

QUESTION 7. Because Jesus gave sight to a blind man on the Sabbath, "some of the Pharisees said, 'This man is not from God, for he does not keep the Sabbath.' But others asked, 'How can a sinner do such miraculous signs?' So they were divided" (Jn 9:16). And yet unlike the blind man, their eyes remained closed, for they refuse to believe the man was blind since birth or that Jesus could be a prophet of God. They press his parents, "How is it that now he can see?" (v. 19) and ask the man the same a second time (v. 24). Their question is instructive, for who could possibly answer *how* this miracle occurred but God alone? Hence, one wonders whether they were seeking the truth or only the answer they wanted. The blind man poses this very thought in his reply in verses 27-33, and the Pharisees angrily throw him out of the synagogue. "Intent, in the pursuit of truth," Ravi Zacharias observes, "is prior to content, or to the availability of it. Author George MacDonald once said, 'To give truth to him who loves it not is only to give him more plentiful reasons for misinterpretation.' The love of truth and the willingness to submit to its demands is the first step" (Ravi Zacharias, *Deliver Us from Evil* [Dallas: Word, 1996], p. 222). We will pursue this idea further in the next study.

QUESTIONS 8-9. "Jesus describes some of the blessings of those who are his sheep. He repeats his earlier teaching that his sheep hear his voice, are known by him, and follow him (v. 27; cf. vv. 3, 4, 14, 16) and have eternal life (v. 28; cf. vv. 9-10). He concludes with dramatic emphasis on the security of his sheep: *no one can snatch them out of my hand* (v. 28). . . . The security of the sheep rests on the shepherd. Jesus' reference to himself as the one able to protect his flock from all dangers is yet another aspect of the incredible claims he is making in this chapter. As always, however, he is not acting on his own apart from the Father: *My Father, who has given them to me, is greater than all; no one can snatch them out of my Father's hand* (v. 29). Again we see the primacy of the Father, the one who these opponents think is their God. In threatening Jesus and his followers they are up against God himself" (Whitacre, *John*, p. 269).

QUESTION 10. As a side note to Jesus' comments here, we should understand "gods" as the word used in Psalm 82:6, which he quotes: they are rulers and judges who God has appointed to lead and serve. Jesus appears to be alluding to this entire brief psalm, which characterizes certain leaders as unjust and blind: "They know nothing, they understand nothing. They walk about in darkness" (v. 5).

STUDY 4

Neutralizing Jesus

JOHN 18:28-40

Purpose: **To show that though one may want to ignore or neutralize Jesus' words, he clearly states, "Everyone on the side of truth listens to me."**

QUESTIONS 1-4. Regarding our ongoing study of the charges against Jesus and the Jewish leadership's expectations of God's Messiah, Lesslie Newbigin astutely observes, "The question of the Jews and the answer of Jesus raise again the fundamental problem of revelation. Jesus has spoken in parables; they demand a plain answer to a straight question: 'Are you the Messiah?' This is to require that Jesus either accept or decline a place already prepared for him in their theology. But Jesus cannot take any place in a true theology except the determinative one. A true theology—that is to say, a true word about God—begins with him who is himself God's word. Jesus has in fact both spoken and acted in such a way that those whom the Father has given him do hear and believe. . . . This is . . . the constant theme of St. John, namely, that to recognize in the man Jesus, in all his weakness, humility, and vulnerability, the very presence of the glory of God can only be the result of a total conversion which none but God can himself bring about. *There is no way by which Jesus can be accommodated within any theology which has its starting point elsewhere. To acknowledge him as who he is, is to accept a shattering of all other structures of confidence and belief,* which is one aspect of what Paul describes as 'being crucified with Christ'" (Newbigin, *Light Has Come,* pp. 131-32, emphasis added).

Additionally, Rodney Whitacre notes, "Pilate asks for the charges against Jesus (v. 29), and from the Jewish leaders' response it seems they were upset by this request: *If he were not a criminal . . . we would not have handed him over to you* (v. 30). They wanted Pilate simply to take their word for it and not begin his own investigation. . . .

"Long before now they had come to the conclusion that Jesus had to be eliminated (7:19-20; 8:40, 44, 59; 10:31; 11:8, 16, 50). This is still their aim, and their specific request of Pilate now becomes clear when they respond that they do not have the right to execute people (v. 31). This could refer to Old Testament prohibitions against killing . . . but more likely it refers to limitations imposed by the Romans. . . . There were occasions when Jews put people to death through mob violence (for example, the stoning of Stephen, Acts 7:58-60). And they were given permission to execute any Gentile, even a Roman, who entered the temple's inner courts. . . . But mob violence has not succeeded against Jesus, and his case is not one for which Rome has given permission for execution. . . . They seem set, however, on having Rome execute Jesus, for then it would be by crucifixion. They probably want him crucified (19:6, 15) not only because it was a particularly brutal and painful form of death, but also because it would signify that Jesus is accursed by God (Deut. 21:23; cf. Gal. 3:13). . . .

"John, however, sees this desire as a fulfillment of Jesus' statement that he would die by being lifted up from the earth (v. 32; 12:32-34)" (Whitacre, *John*, pp. 438-39).

QUESTION 5. Each of the Gospel writers mention the charge of Jesus being "King of the Jews," and Pilate places this title over Jesus when he hangs on the cross (see Jn 19:19-22 for this ironic scene). Attesting again to the reliability of the records about Jesus' life, the charge comes from the life of Jesus, for it is nearly impossible for us to imagine Christians making up a charge that was incapable of fulfillment—Jesus did not become the (political) king of the Jews in Israel. And it no doubt owes its origins to the message of Jesus—*the kingdom of God* (Mk 1:15). The charge implies an enormous claim on Jesus' part, and undoubtedly that claim emerged in the trial before various leaders (see esp. Mk 14:62). It also implies that Jesus thought he had a claim on the entire nation, and this is clearly a part of his choice of twelve disciples who represent the nation Jesus is now establishing. That he was not one of the Twelve, but *over* the Twelve, implies his "kingship" over this new nation. In other words, the charge is grounded historically in Jesus' message and his actions.

QUESTION 6. Pilate is focused on the expedient political question—*Is this man really a king and thus potential enemy of Rome?*—yet Jesus tries to move him to consider the deeper essential reality, "Is that your own idea?" (v. 34). Rodney Whitacre comments, "Jesus neither affirms nor denies his identity as a king, but he responds like a king. He speaks of his kingdom and calmly focuses the attention on Pilate, asking a question that tests Pilate's heart (v. 34). He is speaking to him as a human being, not as the Roman governor. Is he personally engaged, or is this just a formality? . . . Such personal interest is necessary to be able to recognize one come from God and to respond appropriately" (Whitacre, *John*, p. 440).

QUESTIONS 7-8. Ravi Zacharias writes, "Jesus reminded us that ultimately truth is not merely propositional. It is absolutely personified in God. 'In the beginning was the Word . . . and the Word was God . . . full of grace and truth' (John 1:1). In clear distinction to all other ideas and systems, Christianity stands unique. The world of religions points to platitudes or paths; the Scriptures point to Christ. In Him alone is the embodiment of Truth. . . .

"Angered by this intrusion into his inner sanctum of motivational insincerity, Pilate began a momentary exchange ending with those climactic words of Jesus: 'They that are on the side of Truth listen to me.' It is most instructive as one rereads this passage to learn a poignant fact about life as it encounters information. Just as absolute truth is personified in God, so truthfulness is found in a person before it is found in propositions. Truthfulness in the heart is an indispensable prerequisite to knowing what is true in the world of ideas" (Ravi Zacharias, "The Hide and Seek of Truth," *Just Thinking* [spring/summer 1993], available online at www.rzim.org/publications/jttran.php?seqid=10).

Elsewhere, Ravi Zacharias adds, "The fundamental problem Jesus was exposing to Pilate and to the world is not the paucity of available truth; it is more often the hypocrisy of our search. Truthfulness in the heart, said Jesus, precedes truth in the objective realm. *Intent is prior to content.* The most provocative statement Jesus made during that penetrating conversation was that the truthfulness or falsity of an individual's heart was revealed by that person's response to Him. The implication was uncompromising. He was, and is, the truth. What you do with Him reveals more about you than it does about Him" (Ravi Zacharias, *Can Man Live Without God?* [Dallas: Word Publishing, 1994], p. 98).

QUESTION 9. Pilate attempts to neutralize Jesus' direct words to him by countering "What is truth?" In our postmodern culture, this translates as, "Yeah, whatever." Clearly he is not interested in this essential question or a reply from Jesus because he walks out: "With this [question] he went out again to the Jews and said, "I find no basis for a charge against him" (v. 38). But his own resistance and inaction trap him, for the Jewish leadership and the crowd outside the palace insist that he crucify Jesus and release the criminal Barabbas. After having Jesus flogged and beaten, Pilate speaks again with the Jews and learns that Jesus claims to be the Son of God (19:7). "When Pilate heard this he was even more afraid" (19:8). Yet even then and after another exchange with Jesus, he chooses what he deems the expedient path and hands Jesus over to be crucified. Though

Pilate may have been successful in getting rid of Jesus, one wonders if his conversations with Jesus (and moreover, his own guilt) followed him in the days and years to come. Interestingly, Matthew ominously writes, "While Pilate was sitting on the judge's seat, his wife sent him this message: 'Don't have anything to do with that innocent man, for I have suffered a great deal today in a dream because of him" (Mt 27:19). Nevertheless, Pilate chose to ignore his wife's words—and Jesus' also.

STUDY 5

Professing Jesus

LUKE 6:43—7:10

Purpose: **To show that professing Jesus involves obedience, trust and humility.**

QUESTIONS 1-3. Darrell Bock writes, "To judge a tree's fruit, we don't look at one particular moment but at a period of production. The product of the life reflects the heart. The product of our discipleship reflects our inner character, what Jesus calls the treasure of the heart [see Lk 12:34]. The value of our speech and actions is determined by the quality of the soul that produces them. In other words, works are a snapshot of the heart. . . .

"By linking the heart and fruit, Jesus ties together motive and action. Works are ultimately a matter of the heart: the product can never be entirely divorced from the motive, and the presence does not mean the absence of faith!

"In fact, the major issue in the life of the disciple is faithfulness. So Jesus issues a challenge in verse 46: '*Why do you call me "Lord, Lord," and do not do what I say?*' The rhetorical question raises the issue of faithfulness. A good heart is faithful, while a hypocritical one is not. Obedience is not a matter of rule keeping but faithfulness. How can one recognize Jesus' authority and call him Lord and then not follow through on the commitment to walk with him.

"With this question Jesus turns to the issue of authority. *He is not formulating some ethic that we could not follow independent of a relationship with him. Having a relationship with him is at the base of faithfulness"* (Bock, *Luke*, p. 129, emphasis added).

QUESTION 4. When we come to the Gospel accounts the term *Lord* is used with a certain degree of emphasis for a miracle-worker. When the centurion needs healing for his servant, he addresses Jesus as "Lord" (Mt 8:6, 8). When his disciples think they are about to perish in a storm, they call Jesus "Lord" (Mt 8:25).

The disciples and followers of Jesus use this term when requesting information or permission. In so doing, the connotation of *Lord* begins to touch on "rabbi" and "teacher." Peter thinks Jesus won't die, slipping in this comment with a prefatory "Lord" (16:22). It is also Peter who asks Jesus a question about a parable and addresses Jesus with "Lord" (Lk 12:41). Nothing in the Synoptic Gospels compares, however, with the extent to which Thomas goes in calling Jesus "My Lord and my God" (Jn 20:28).

QUESTION 5. The term *Lord* emerges from a *relationship* with Jesus. Jesus was not a master or teacher whom one would never have a conversation with or get to know (such as a corporate boss or lecturer in a large university). In fact, throughout the Gospels we observe Jesus taking time to build relationship, whether with his disciples, the woman at the well (Jn 4), or even—in a large crowd pressing him—with a woman who touches him (see e.g., Lk 8:42-48). It is difficult for us now to think our way back into the minds of Jesus' followers to see just how much exaltedness is latent in the term *Lord.* I find it possible that with this term the disciples labeled Jesus with a title that revealed that they thought Jesus was more than a prophet and more than a typical teacher.

Typical teachers were also not often called "Messiah." This Hebrew term, translated into Greek with *christos* (Christ), was used for those who were "anointed" for some special task. We've got only one piece of evidence that followers of Jesus called Jesus "Messiah" during his lifetime, and the witnesses vary in specific wording:

Mark 8:29:   You are the Messiah.

Matthew 16:16:   You are the Messiah, the Son of the living God.

Luke 9:20:   You are the Messiah of God.

The core, of course, is the confession that Jesus is the Messiah. And the confession was at the very heart of early Christian belief about Jesus (e.g., Mt 1:1; Mk 1:1; Jn 1:17; Acts 2:36; Rom 1:1; 10:4, 17; Heb 9:11; Jas 1:1; 1 Pet 1:1; 5:10; 1 Jn 1:3; Rev 1:1).

Early Christians could have chosen several terms to label Jesus, but this label was chosen to be up front and close. Other labels were used—*Lord, Son of God, Savior*—but no term stuck so closely to Jesus as this one—so close, in fact, that it became a personal name: Jesus Christ (not Jesus, who is the Messiah). It is an irony that Jesus' favorite name for himself, "Son of Man," was quickly dropped and almost never used by others for Jesus. The label *Christ* stuck because it told the "Christian story" the best. And that story was that the Creator and Covenant God had brought to fulfillment all his plans and promises when Jesus performed his ministry on earth. The Christian story, then, is a Messianic rendition of Jewish history.

QUESTION 7. As a background note, Matthew 8:5-13 is the parallel passage to this story with a slight difference: Matthew says that the centurion speaks to Jesus directly, whereas Luke features his friends who speak on his behalf. Bible scholar Leon Morris suggests that we "see Matthew as abbreviating the story and leaving out details inessential to his purpose. What a man does through his agents he may be said to do himself. So Matthew simply gives the gist of the centurion's communication to Jesus, whereas Luke in greater detail gives the actual sequence of events. Perhaps we can discern something of the differing purposes of the two Evangelists in their treatment of the messengers. Matthew was concerned primarily with the centurion's faith and nationality; to him the messengers were irrelevant, even a distraction. But Luke was interested in the man's character and specifically in his humility: to him the messengers were a vital part of the story" (Leon Morris, *Luke*, Tyndale New Testament Commentaries [Downers Grove, Ill.: InterVarsity Press, 1994], p. 151).

Regarding Jesus' response to the centurion, Darrell Bock observes, "Jesus reacts emotionally (this is one of the few places where Luke records Jesus' emotion): he is *amazed*. Jesus is said to be amazed only here, in Matthew's parallel account (Mt. 8:10) and in Mark 6:6, where he is astonished at unbelief. Jesus turns and issues his commendation: *'I have not found such great faith even in Israel!'* The statement is like a neon light. Here is faith that should be emulated. Here is trust, confidence, rest in the authority of God and awareness of his plan. The Jewish nation, and all others, can learn from this outsider. Aware of Jesus' authority, the centurion has committed the well-being of his beloved slave into Jesus' hands. Jesus commends the centurion's humility and his understanding of Jesus' authority: such faith is exemplary.

Returning home, the messengers find the slave healthy. The request has been granted, the slave restored. Jesus' commendation must resonate even more powerfully as they contemplate the miracle. Surely if such faith is possible outside of Israel, it can happen anywhere. Furthermore, it is clear that Jesus possesses a unique authority: he does not need to be physically present to bring about what he wills" (Bock, *Luke*, pp. 133-34).

STUDY 6

Following Jesus

MATTHEW 6:25-34; 7:7-12

Purpose: **To show that following Jesus involves surrendering ourselves to him.**

QUESTIONS 1-4. Throughout the Sermon on the Mount, Jesus uses both positive and negative imperative verbs (or commands) that engage his listeners' attention: *love, pray, do not judge*. He says, "Do not worry" (v. 25), and instructs us to "look" and "see" (vv. 26, 28). In doing so he exhorts us to have his heavenly Father's perspective: seek *him* and *he* will provide.

Twice in this passage—and significantly, *eleven times* in chapter 6 alone—Jesus invites the listener to understand God as "your heavenly Father" (or "your Father"). Jesus describes his Father's tender care for his creation: He feeds the birds and makes the flowers grow. "Are you not much more valuable than they?" Jesus asks. He makes another lesser-to-greater comparison in 7:9-11 when he rhetorically asks, "How much more will your Father in heaven give good gifts to those who ask him."

Commenting on the parallel passage found in Luke 12:22-31, Darrell Bock writes, "Jesus explains his call away from worry by noting that life is more than food or clothing. The deepest dimension of life is relationship with God and with others. . . . Jesus made it clear that real life has to do with relationship. Living is more than having; it is being in relationship with God and relating well to others. Placing concern for our daily needs in God's hands is part of what it means to have relationship with God."

Regarding Jesus' instruction not to worry, Bock suggests, "If worrying is futile in adding even a small increment to your lifespan, *why do you worry about the rest?* Worry is wasted energy, an emotional investment that yields nothing. Worry actually reflects the tension we have when we feel that life is out of our control; it is the product of feeling isolated in the creation. Disciples, however, should know that God cares for them. Biblically, the opposite of worry is trust. That is why after offering some more illustrations Jesus addresses his audience as *you of little faith*. . . . He wants them to come to trust God again" (Bock, *Luke,* pp. 227-28).

QUESTION 7. "Unlike those in the world who consume themselves with the pursuit of food and clothing, disciples are to focus on seeking God's kingdom. This means we pursue relationship with God, his will and the evidence of his rule and guidance in our lives as we seek to serve him. Matthew 6:33 [says] to pursue God's kingdom is to pursue his righteousness. Jesus offers a promise with the exhortation: God will provide these other things as well. We can major on what God desires for us because he is committed to our care" (Bock, *Luke*, pp. 228-29). Indeed, Jesus promises that his heavenly Father will not only provide for our needs ("what you will eat or drink") but bless us with "good gifts" as well when we seek him and his kingdom.

"Jesus describes as righteous those who conform to God's will as revealed both in the Old Testament and in his own teachings. The foundation for Jesus' teachings on righteous behavior is that the kingdom of God has been inaugurated in his own person and ministry (Luke 7:18-23; 11:20). Since God's kingdom is a righteous kingdom when Jesus inaugurates the kingdom he brings righteousness to pass and expects righteous behavior from his followers. . . .

"From the evidence of the Gospels, Jesus' teaching stressed that his followers must conform their lives to God's will. Thus it may be argued that the idea of righteousness, if not the terminology, is found everywhere in the teachings of Jesus: in his demand for repentance, in his blessings for good works, in his practice of social mercy and in his consistent concern for personal holiness. . . .

"In using his own teachings as the basis for righteousness, Jesus reveals that the OT Law and Prophets (Mt 5:17) are being fulfilled in his own teachings and that he is the Messiah. . . . Jesus fulfills the Law and so reveals a new standard of conduct (Mt 5:20). Henceforth, the righteousness of God's people is determined by conformity to the teachings of Jesus, which in turn fulfill the Old Testament revelation of God's will.

. . . Again, this righteousness is not an outward conformity to the Law or an appeal to ritual observances, but the necessary fruit of commitment to Jesus as Messiah and Lord. The link between commitment and obedience is illustrated by Jesus' words at the end of the Sermon on the Mount: 'Everyone then who hears these words of mine and does them' (Mt 7:21-27)" (Scot McKnight, "Justice, Righteousness," in *Dictionary of Jesus and the Gospels,* ed. Joel B. Green, Scot McKnight and I. Howard Marshall [Downers Grove, Ill.: InterVarsity Press 1992], p. 413).

QUESTION 8. Ravi Zacharias observes, "It is impossible, when dealing with all of reality, to force mathematical certainty into every test for truthfulness. Life is just not livable that way, and in fact, science would collapse if it consistently believed that at every step. Einstein himself challenged this illusory certainty in mathematics, saying, 'As far as the propositions of mathematics refer to reality, they are not certain; and as far as they are certain, they do not refer to reality.' It would be better to describe our pursuit as that which seeks a high degree of certainty, or meaningful certainty. A meaningful and high degree of certainty, rather than mathematical certainty, is more attainable. . . .

"Having said that, it is equally important for the pursuer of truth who approaches life purely from one's sense perception to observe the same caution. If the telescope proved anything, it warned us of the erroneous perceptual assumptions that we can make if perception reigns supreme, for it does not always reveal things as they are. . . .

"Let me borrow an illustration from Francis Schaeffer. . . . Suppose you were to leave a room with two glasses on the table, Glass A and Glass B. Glass A has two ounces of water in it, and Glass B is empty. When you return at the end of the day, Glass B now has water in it and Glass A is empty. You could assume that someone took the water from Glass A and put it into Glass B. That, however, does not fully explain the situation, because you notice that Glass B has four ounces of water in it, whereas

Glass A had only two ounces in it when you left in the morning.

"You are confronted with a problem that at best has only a partial explanation. Whether the water from Glass A was poured into Glass B is debatable. But what is beyond debate is that all of the water in Glass B could not have come from Glass A. The additional two ounces had to have come from elsewhere.

"God has put enough into the world to make faith in Him a most reasonable thing, and he has left enough out to make it impossible to live by sheer reason or observation alone. Science may be able to explain the two ounces in Glass B. It cannot explain the four ounces in it" (Ravi Zacharias, *The Real Face of Atheism* [Grand Rapids: Baker, 2004], pp. 110-12).

QUESTION 9. Regarding the distinctiveness of the Christian faith as relationship with God, Ravi Zacharias says, "Christianity stands in stark contrast to everything that other worldviews affirm and assert. . . . True power is being expressed in the cross—restraint, mercy, forgiveness—all when the very One who is offering those things had the capacity to counter instead with force and with domination.

"In contrast, consider the radicals in the Islamic movement, for whom power is always present, always political, always military and always violent. The cross will always be a stumbling block to them because it challenges the very core of their thinking. Jesus' way is completely different from theirs. In Jesus' way, winning comes through love and a change of heart. . . .

"It is through the empowering of the Holy Spirit that we are able to see this change. Once I understand that the cross was a personal provision for the sin of every man and every woman, I can identify with Christ in the fact that this is *my* Savior taking *my* guilt and *my* penalty. Then, when I confess my sin, receive Him and trust Him, the Bible says that He comes and dwells within me.

"We hear so little of this indwelling today, so little of 'Christ in you,

the hope of glory' [Col 1:27]. We have talked so much of accepting and
receiving that we have forgotten the intimacy with which He comes and
dwells within us. There is no other world religion or worldview that
talks in those terms.

"In Islam, Allah is seen as distant and totally transcendent. In Bud-
dhism, there is no god. In the core of Hindu thinking, you are, in effect,
made to become god. But in the Christian faith, there is the nearness of
God. We do not go to the Temple anymore to worship; we take the temple with us. This body is the temple of the living God. There is commun-
ion; there is intimacy. We understand that this body is where God wishes
to make His residence, and we see the sacredness of the human body"
(Ravi Zacharias, "A Conversation with Ravi Zacharias and Jim Dailey,"
Just Thinking [spring/summer 2002], available at www.rzim.org/publica-
tions/jttran.php?seqid=83).

QUESTIONS 10-11. Similar to his instruction in Luke 6:25-28, Jesus
again encourages his listeners with three imperatives: *ask, seek* and
knock. Just as the one who seeks his kingdom and righteousness is prom-
ised that "all these things will be given to you as well," so "he who seeks
finds." As noted earlier, Jesus makes a lesser-to-greater comparison, this
time between an earthly father and our heavenly Father. In calling the
father "evil," Jesus acknowledges his sinfulness but does not emphasize
it; rather, he uses it for effect to note that if a fallen human provides for
his child, how much more will God take care of his children.

Of the parallel passage in Luke 11:9-13, in which Jesus characterizes
"good gifts" as "the Holy Spirit," Darrell Bock writes, "In the context of
the Lord's Prayer, Jesus is asking the disciples to pursue both the spiritual
goals and the request for basic needs indicated in the earlier prayer with
great boldness. . . . All we need to do is ask, seek and knock. These are
not blank-check promises that God will give us anything we want, but
promises that requests for our spiritual welfare will be heard. . . .

"As the disciples bring their spiritual requests to the Father, they know that he is ready to help them. He longs to work in them and supply the Spirit for their needs. Like a father who feeds his child, so the Father will supply his disciples with the Spirit whey they needed to be guided. . . . At the foundation of all discipleship is trust in the Father's goodness. He loves to provide for all our spiritual needs" (Bock, *Luke,* p. 207).